THANKSLIVING

THANKSLIVING

A Turkey's Tale

DR. M. DAVID CHAMBERS

DDC 4 Him Productions

CONTENTS

Thanksliving

Tom Morrow

Be Thankful

The Real Story

More by Author

~ 1 ~

"AN UNFULFILLING CHILLING"

Agitated. Uneasy. Weary. Faith was anything but restful. Though she had been excited when her husband, Dairs insisted that she take a "mental day" to recuperate from the busy weeks they had lived through recently, she simply could not relax. Though she and her family absolutely loved being on the run to; cookouts, celebrations, speaking engagements and family gatherings, the past few weeks had been more intense than most. She couldn't remember the last home-cooked meal they had enjoyed, and for Faith, time around the dinner table with her

"3 men" was priceless. Though the little cabin she called home looked "just fine" in her husband's assessment, she found it hard to settle for, "just fine", and wanted time to clean it up to her standards. Then there was all that had to be done in the days ahead. Clearly this little lady needed a breather. Dairs had realized she was overwhelmed and attempted to "set the stage" for a peaceful day at home; a cider-scented candle blazing away on the table beside her accompanied by a piping hot cup of her favorite wild-berry tea, and shortbread cookies neatly stacked on an old plate, all to promote relaxation while she curled up under her favorite fleece blanket with one of her Amish novels at the window seat of their cabin in the woods. If this weren't enough, she had the quiet of a cool Autumn Day and a gentle breeze assisting the flaming red, brilliant gold, striking orange and even some occasional green leaves as they danced together in the front yard, to soothe her. The only sound that could be heard was the occasional rattle of a cooled fireplace coal dug from the hearth by her new kitten being batted around the living room floor. Gazing out the window she saw Dairs, and her boys, Nolan and Michael hop into the truck and head out for the day to run errands and give her the house all to herself. Truly this had the makings of a genuinely tranquil day, all she had to do was just chill. Even though she wanted to get up and get to work, she knew she needed a break, and this was her chance to relax, recharge and renew for the Holidays ahead. Why then, was she so restless? Letting out a sigh and letting her book fall from her hands, she laid her head back and closed her eyes in contemplative thought.

~ 2 ~

"THE DULL SIDE"

As she lay on the couch thinking, she almost drifted off to dream, but seeing her foot move under the blanket, the kitten attacked with a vengeance. After shaking the ferocious little feline loose from the death grip it had on her toes, Faith sat up a bit and seemed to have one of those "ah ha moments" where the light bulb comes on and you finally have something come into focus.

"I know what the problem is," she quipped out loud. "Everyone is always telling you to look at the bright side, all the while ignoring the dull side!" "I have to run, run, run all the time, doing so many things for so many others (who often don't even seem appreciative) and there are just so many responsibilities I can't even catch my breath." Allowing gloom to set in she began to play over all that was going on in the world around her, and how dire everything seemed, especially if you even glanced at the latest headlines. She lamented over how divided people were becoming, along with all the health concerns that she knew of just within her own sphere of influence, and went further and further down the rabbit-hole of pessimism and negativity. Over the next few moments this young lady who was typically; fun-loving, care-free, and a genuine ray of sunshine, allowed herself to drift into utter despair. "Bright side my eye, and it's only going to get worse, Thanksgiving is just around the corner!" The very words she had spoken shocked even her. She had never had the slightest disdain for the Holiday before. In fact, she had enjoyed it. Almost snapping out of her unhappiness, she thought about how much she enjoyed cooking and being with family, but a second wave of self-pity washed over her and drug her back in to the deep. "What is Thanksgiving anyway but "Christmas Lite", all the work and none of the gifts!" "People will be expecting fried pies, my cranberry salad, turkey and gravy, cakes, etc., and I bet I won't even be able to get the right ingredients this year with the way the stores are stocked." "Even if I can find the time and ingredients, I bet that old mixer chooses this year to die, and heaven-forbid if Dairs uses that old turkey fryer, and he's such a turkey himself." Though completely out of character for this naturally soft-spoken, level-headed lady, Faith yells out, "what have I got to be thankful for anyway!" She slumps down under cover of the blanket and cries herself to sleep.

~ 3 ~

"WRECKED"

RINNNNNGGGGGG,RINNNNNNGGGGGG, RINNNNNNGGGGGG. Her phone jarred her from a much-needed deep sleep, such as she had not had in a while. Looking at the caller ID she sees it's a friend from the local coffee shop, she attempts to shake herself to clarity and then answers. The voice on the other end of the line seemed strained, "Hello Missy, this is Melinda, have you heard from Dairs in the last few minutes?" Trying to sound chipper despite the events of the morning and not wanting to let on she was asleep in the middle of the day, she mustered up her strongest voice and replied, "not since this morning, why?" Having no idea she was about to get the answer to the question she fell asleep to, ("what do I have to be thankful for anyway?") she eagerly awaited an answer. "Well, it may not be him, but I just passed a terrible accident uptown and it looked like his Dodge pickup, but I can't be sure, it's pretty messed up." The words engulfed her like a heavy fog, and she nearly fell off the couch trying to untangle herself from the blanket. Faith began frantically dialing her husbands cell number in hopes of finding he was nowhere near the accident. No answer. "I'll try Nolan's cell", she thought. No answer. Her heart was pounding like a kettle drum in her chest and she began to feel dizzy. Grabbing her keys, she thought to rush to the scene and see for herself, but realizing she was in no condition to drive she called her best friend, Renee to seek prayer and help. Frantically attempting to convey what had happened to her friend, she breaks down on the phone, "hurry please!" After throwing shoes on in order to be ready, and attempting to call her beloved numerous times, she begins rummaging through her husband's desk to find out how to reach the emergency response system built into Dairs truck. She finds a folder labeled, "Important Documents". She begins leafing through the various documents and is further distressed by the life insurance policies, and "final wishes" she finds. Flinging the folder across the room, she looks down to see an old tattered piece of loose-leaf notebook paper coming to rest from the flurry of papers she had launched. As she opens the paper, she realizes it is written in her own handwriting. There in her husbands' "Important Documents" was a homework assignment she had done in the 8th grade-what seemed like a lifetime ago. The assignment came rushing back to her, she was tasked with writing a paper on what she wanted her life to look like in 5 years. Realizing she could do nothing until her friend arrived, she began to read. Her already tear-laden eyes welled up as she read making it difficult to see, but she plowed through the letter now saturated with her liquid emotion.

"DON'T KNOW WHAT YOU'VE GOT UNTIL IT'S GONE"

"Everything I ever wished for came true...and now it could be gone forever. God, I am so sorry for being so foolish." The broken-hearted wife and mother was now more settled because the shock of what might be reality set in. Praying aloud, she startled the kitten who didn't know what to think of all these emotions, "Even in 8th grade as a pre-teen, I knew I wanted a good husband who drove a truck, boys, a log cabin, and to be a homemaker. God, you have blessed me with all that, and so much more. How could I have been so blind to the blessings in my life; my husband, my children, a roof over my head, food on the table, a great family, a wonderful church family and community, my health and so much more?" She begged forgiveness for allowing an unseen enemy to creep into her mind and draw her down into the dismal depths of despair and thanklessness. She begged her Creator to please spare her husband and sons, and whoever else might have been in the accident. She begged for another chance to prove to God, her family and community that she absolutely adored them all and loved serving them more than anything in life. She pleaded with raw emotion and a genuine, contrite heart for so many things, even minuscule things like the chance to see if the mixer would finally break this year, and for the opportunity to go "hunting" for the ingredients to cook her specialties for her beloved family and friends. Faith even asked for the chance to see her husband make a huge mess with the turkey fryer as he always did. This prayer warrior who arose early every morning to pray for those in her life, now prayed even harder than ever before. Before she could say Amen, the door flung open and Renee came rushing to her friends' side. Once again, the flood gates opened and Faith wept on her friends' strong shoulder. Renee held her tight and helped her cry a bit, but then pushed her to arm's length while firmly holding Faith's shoulders and looking her square in the eyes. "Okay girl, now let's pull ourselves together and do what we can. You have told me so many times to have faith, now it's your turn! It's time to be exactly who your name says you are..." The two grabbed a few tissues, put on their "brave faces" and headed out the door.

~ 5 ~

"TURKEY CALL"

RINNNNNGGGGGG,RINNNNNNGGGGGG, RINNNNNNGGGGGG. The phone startles her and she nearly flings it out the window pulling it from her purse. Heart racing, she flips the phone over and gasps as she sees the name on the caller ID. There on the screen, underneath her favorite picture of her husband with his cheesy grin, she sees the word, "Dairs". Answering the phone she holds her breath, hoping it really is her hubby rather than someone else who has picked up his phone at the wreck. Though this husband of hers could truly be a turkey at times and aggravate her to no end, never before had she been so happy to hear the words, "Hey Babe." For the first time all day, she breathed a genuine sigh of peace and relief. Dairs goes on to say, "first let me assure you we are all ok." Though Dairs would go on to tell her all the details of the wreck and how his precious truck was totaled, she heard little after those words. What mattered to her was that her family was intact, and she would once again get to "hug her blessings". This was one "turkey call" she would never forget.

~ 6 ~

"THANKSLIVING"

Though her "mental day" had turned into one of the craziest of her life, Faith was at peace like never before. There was really no logical reason her husband and boys should have walked away from the mangled truck without even a scratch. When she finally saw the vehicle, she shuddered to think what might have been. Faith would go on to have the very best Thanksgiving of her life. Using the excuse, "we have one less car for right now" she goaded Dairs into going with her shopping for all the ingredients they needed for her cooking spree, and even talked him into buying extra so she could make for friends and family that they weren't even eating with. She spent hours in the kitchen in the days to follow, filling their home with the delectable smells of sweets and main dishes too delicious to describe. As she worked feverishly to get things done, Dairs couldn't help but notice that his bride seemed to have a little more spring in her step, as she seemed to float along from task to task with great joy, even humming her favorite songs as she did. Though she had missed out on a relaxing day that it seemed she needed so sorely, she had come to realize that joy, satisfaction and thankfulness in life is truly a matter of focus. Sure, there are always some tough things going on in life, but we cannot lose focus on the FACT that there is far more good, if we will just open our eyes to see it. Further, she determined in her heart to have complete faith in God as He provided for her what He felt was best. Finally, this sweet lady resolved to live in the spirit of **Philippians 2:14** and never be drawn into whining and complaining again. Faith celebrated a true Thanksgiving that year and in all the years to follow as she lived out a life of pure gratitude in Thanksliving.

Yesterday is a memory, tomorrow is a hope, today is the present-a gift. Don't wait for a tomorrow (that may never come) to enjoy the gift and beauty of today. When life gets you down, a sure-fire way to get back to Thanksliving is to, "Count your blessings, name them one by one, and it will surprise you what the Lord hath done!"

Happy Thanksgiving!

Psalm 100

"O taste and see that the Lord is good:
blessed is the man that trusteth in him."
Psalm 34:8

POEMS OF THE SEASON

Thanksliving

Life's never-ending struggle,
makes it easy to be,
Discouraged and downtrodden,
Frustrated and so weary.
This world with all its darkness,
Makes it hard to see,
The blessings that surround us,
God's grace to you and me.
So, when you feel disheartened,
And sadness takes it hold,
Count your many blessings,
Worth more than purest gold;
Family, friends and so much more,
We have from God's great giving,
This truth plus His eternal love,
Should drive us to Thanksliving.

Dr. M. David Chambers 2021

Tom Morrow

There once was a turkey named Tom,
Who lived on a beautiful Farm,
Tom was quite smart, he'd mastered the art,
Of avoiding bodily harm.
Each year as November drew near,
This Turkey would act quite unwell,
He'd stumble and trip, swoon and slip,
When the farmer would look he fell.
Yes, Tom was quite the smart bird,
A genius some may have said,
Not only was he not eaten,
In fact, he got fed instead.
The Farmer was never the wiser,
Each year ate dinner with sorrow,
He just never quite knew how,
Tom was always better on the morrow.

Dr. M. David Chambers 2021

Be Thankful

Be thankful that you don't already have everything you desire,
If you did, what would there be to look forward to?
Be thankful when you don't know something
For it gives you the opportunity to learn.
Be thankful for the difficult times.
During those times you grow.
Be thankful for your limitations
Because they give you opportunities for improvement.
Be thankful for each new challenge
Because it will build your strength and character.
Be thankful for your mistakes
They will teach you valuable lessons.

Be thankful when you're tired and weary
Because it means you've made a difference.
It is easy to be thankful for the good things.
A life of rich fulfillment comes to those who are
also thankful for the setbacks.
GRATITUDE can turn a negative into a posi-
tive.
Find a way to be thankful for your troubles
and they can become your blessings.

Author Unknown

The Real Story

Psalm 100

1 Make a joyful noise unto the Lord, all ye lands. [2] Serve the Lord with gladness: come before his presence with singing. [3] Know ye that the Lord he is God: it is he that hath made us, and not we ourselves; we are his people, and the sheep of his pasture. [4] Enter into his gates with thanksgiving, and into his courts with praise: be thankful unto him, and bless his name. [5] For the Lord is good; his mercy is everlasting; and his truth endureth to all generations.

Jeremiah 17:7-8

[7] Blessed is the man that trusteth in the Lord, and whose hope the Lord is. [8] For he shall be as a tree planted by the waters, and that spreadeth out her roots by the river, and shall not see

when heat cometh, but her leaf shall be green; and shall not be careful in the year of drought, neither shall cease from yielding fruit.

Matthew 6:30-33

[30] Wherefore, if God so clothe the grass of the field, which to day is, and to morrow is cast into the oven, shall he not much more clothe you, O ye of little faith?[31] Therefore take no thought, saying, What shall we eat? or, What shall we drink? or, Wherewithal shall we be clothed?[32] (For after all these things do the Gentiles seek:) for your heavenly Father knoweth that ye have need of all these things.[33] But seek ye first the kingdom of God, and his righteousness; and all these things shall be added unto you.

James 1:17

[17] Every good gift and every perfect gift is from above, and cometh down from the Father of lights, with whom is no variableness, neither shadow of turning.

Philippians 4:19

¹⁹ But my God shall supply all your need according to his riches in glory by Christ Jesus.

The Beginning

More by Author

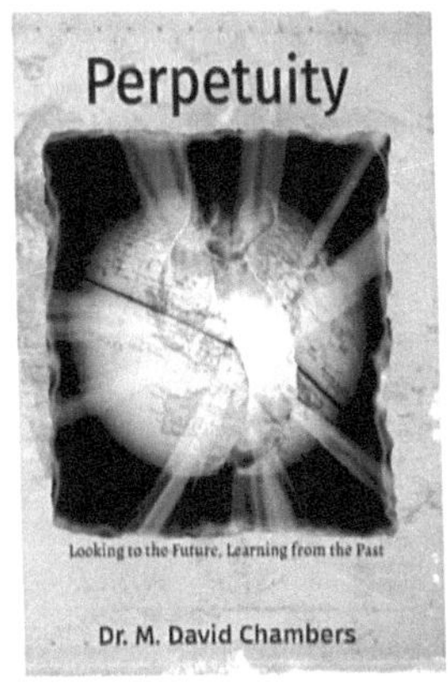

www.ingramcontent.com/pod-product-compliance
Lightning Source LLC
Chambersburg PA
CBHW032133050726

47590CB00008B/3074